Edward Hungerford

Centennial Sermons on the History of the Center

Congregational Church,

of Meriden, Conn., preached in that church Sundays, October 1st and 22d,

1876

Edward Hungerford

Centennial Sermons on the History of the Center Congregational Church,
of Meriden, Conn., preached in that church Sundays, October 1st and 22d, 1876

ISBN/EAN: 9783337113940

Printed in Europe, USA, Canada, Australia, Japan

Cover: Foto ©Lupo / pixelio.de

More available books at **www.hansebooks.com**

CENTENNIAL SERMONS

ON THE HISTORY OF

THE CENTER CONGREGATIONAL CHURCH,

OF

MERIDEN, CONN.,

PREACHED IN THAT CHURCH

SUNDAYS, OCTOBER 1ST AND 22D, 1876,

BY

EDWARD HUNGERFORD,

PASTOR OF THE CHURCH.

———•———

HARTFORD:

PRESS OF THE CASE, LOCKWOOD & BRAINARD COMPANY.

1877.

SERMON.

ZECHARIAH 4:10. "For who hath despised the day of small things?"

I AM going to lead you back, my friends, this afternoon, to the day of small things. In a very hasty way—altogether too hasty a way, I propose that we follow, through nearly one hundred and fifty years, the path which the feet of your fathers have worn into the soil, until that path brings us to this place where we worship to-day.

It seems to me especially fitting that the pastor of this church should go back into those early years. The history of neither of the Congregational churches in this city can be complete without those antecedents, out of which the life of both has sprung. As two branches of one family, now living apart, but with no family feuds between them, we hail and venerate a common ancestry, as we hold to one and the same Congregational polity, in which we serve one Lord.

But more than this: I should not be true to the position which your love assigns me, as pastor of this church, if I were to forget that the small beginnings of all the church life in all Meriden centered a century and a half ago in a place not far from this spot; that it was all removed hither soon after the close of the first quarter of a century; so that right around this old homestead cluster the traditions of over a hundred and twenty years. Hither your fathers and grandfathers and great-grandfathers have turned their faces Sabbath after Sabbath, from generation to generation. Here, within the sound of my voice, a whole line of pastors, in unbroken succession, has preached the gospel. First, Hall, then Hubbard, and Willard, and Ripley, and Hinsdale, and Perkins, and Stevens, and so on down the line. To this place, in the olden time, the bodies of your fathers and your mothers were brought for the last service on earth, before they were borne to that wind-swept graveyard on yonder hill, or to that still nearer one under the trees. On this very spot many of you who no longer worship here, were baptized; and here many of you stood when you first named the name of Christ. Around this place have gathered, in the last century and a quarter, the rumors and excitements of our country's great and terrible wars, and the news of many battles has been discussed in this center, to which the people gathered in all times of great commotion. Here great questions of public policy have been discussed from the pulpit, and the discussion has been prolonged by the people; while around these very doors the passions of men have raged in open-handed violence, over which at last right has triumphed and peace has spread her wings.

Oh, sacred spot! Oh, holy and hallowed memories! Lift up your heads, dear friends, in the just pride of such traditions, and fail not to honor the very dust whereon your church is built as dust consecrated by the feet which have trodden it, and by the stirring memories which history has written in it for ever.

Let us turn, then, to the day of small things.

On the closing Sunday of October, one hundred and forty-seven years ago this month, at the hour of morning service, you might have seen a little mixed company of young and elderly people gathering on the southwestern slope of yonder height, which we still call " Meeting-house Hill," and gravely stepping in family knots from under the trees (which in this season are clothed in colors caught from the sunsets,) into a little church, only thirty feet by thirty, no larger, therefore than many a country school-house. But they came out from under the autumnal glory into the glory of the house of the Lord. It was a very precious house to them : built out of hardy sacrifices with sturdy toil.

It is very still up here on this Sunday morning ; if, perchance, it is one of our gentler October days. There has been no sound of a bell to break the quiet. Steeple or bell this house has none. There has been no clatter of carriages ; these people have come on foot, or at best on horseback,—a father in the saddle, with a mother and child mounted on the pillion behind ; or, perhaps, a father walking by the side of his horse while the whole family cling to the saddle and the mother's skirts. Far away to the south the old home settlement of their fathers in Wallingford street caught their eyes as they turned to enter the house of God, and the whole country was bathed in rest.

Inside the church, these fathers and mothers, in

1*

plain homespun, or possibly, in case of some mother
—if the vanity of the world and the temptation
of so public a place were too much to be resisted
—in a silk gown which had been *her* mother's, were
ranged on benches, the women on one side and the
men on the other, in grave rows, waiting in silence
for the service to begin.

In that service there is neither organ nor choir.
The singing is congregational. The whole service is
simple and earnest, consisting of prayers and hymns
and spiritual songs, and the preaching from a text.

I was going to say—together with the reading of the
word—but it is a singular fact that at this time " in
New England reading a chapter in the Bible," as a
set form, "in public worship, was looked upon as a long
step in the direction of a liturgy ;" and our fathers
hated liturgies as a relic of popery. " Dr. Hopkins,
who ventured upon the dangerous feat (of reading the
Scriptures in public worship), during his ministry in
Western Massachusetts, (1743—1769) brought on
himself a storm of opposition."

It was a small beginning, but to one who has seen
anything of the frontier life of our national growth,
the picture which I give you here is only the oft-re-
peated story of the first church built in many a new
settlement, during the past two hundred years, with
like toil, and in like simplicity, and holding, for a
shorter or longer period, a like simple worship. There
is, however, this difference. At that time the primi-
tive character of worship was insisted on as matter
of principle. The circumstance and show of our
modern worship have won their way, through much
opposition, against the older methods.

These people who sit waiting in this October stillness for the service to begin, are people of other habits, and other thoughts in many respects, from ourselves. We differ from them in some things which touch the religious life, and in some of these things we differ for the worse. But, after all, we are more like them in religion than in anything else. To the essentials of their religious faith, and to the spirit of their church polity, and to their ideas of religious liberty, we still hold. But in matters of state the change has been revolutionary. These fathers and mothers of ours are true and loyal subjects of King George the second. They are Englishmen in near descent, and are proud of being under the English king.

The mother country is the center of their civil life and thought, and in the prayer which will soon go up to heaven, our gracious sovereign the king of these colonies will, no doubt, be conscientiously and loyally remembered.

The republic has not yet been born. The Declaration of Independence is still nearly fifty years in the dim future, not yet thought of by one of these loyal subjects of the throne, as even a remote possibility. The wise policy of the adviser of King George in fostering the trade of the colonies, and avoiding taxation, was delaying the day of struggle, and, although in discussion about matters of royal prerogative, and rights of trade, the jealousy of England was sometimes manifested in hinted fears lest by fostering the numbers and wealth of the inhabitants of the colonies they "were creating formidable antagonists to

English industry, and nursing a disposition to rebellion," nevertheless, at this time neither rebellion nor a republic had been born in the thought even of the colonies. At this moment the thoughts of these fathers went in politics little beyond such matters, as the attempt of England here in Connecticut, to perpetuate the English laws of inheritance in favor of the oldest son; or, in religion, they were occupied with the church difficulty, now going on among their neighbors in Guilford, over the Rev. Thomas Ruggles; or in politics, again, with the strife, at that time prolonged in Massachusetts, between the General Assembly and the Crown about the salary of the governor whom England sent over to look after her interests in that colony.

If I seem to go out of my way to speak of these things here, it is because the simple mention of the date at which this church began its life conveys nothing to our minds except the element of time. That which concerns us is to know what those fathers were thinking of, and how they lived in the days of small things. We must connect the date with the social, political, and religious circumstances which alone constituted the founding of a church, an important event, and which introduce us to the daily life of the people we commemorate.

In regard to religion, these fathers stood on the eve of great events which were powerfully to affect their religious life.

Previous to this time our churches had been much engaged with the forms of church government. But history tells us that both in this country and in England, the spirit of piety, and the practical religious life had greatly declined.

One of your former pastors, Mr. Perkins, says, we may conclude with almost entire certainty, that Meriden did not differ much in these respects from the rest of New England. But a change was coming. One month later, that is, in November of this same year, John Wesley, in England, then twenty-six years old, joined his brother Charles at Oxford, where the Holy Club was formed, and the foundations of that great movement which has made Wesley's name revered and loved throughout the Christian world, were baptized by the name of Methodist. Another man, who was destined to exert a mighty influence on our American churches, George Whitefield, lacked at this time, but one month of being fifteen years of age, and in eleven years more, or in 1740, at the early age of twenty-six, he was to preach to vast crowds in the cities and villages of Massachusetts, Rhode Island, and Connecticut. Here also, in this same month of October, in this little church on Meeting House Hill, or more likely from the steps in front of it, owing to the crowds which everywhere came together when he spoke, he was to stir the religious thought and heart of Meriden.

One more man, whose name was to be identified with the great religious awakening, soon to come over the churches, Jonathan Edwards, was also at this time, and in this month of October, twenty-six years old. Two years earlier, he had been settled at Northampton, where, under his preaching, was to begin only six years from the founding of our church, that series of revivals, whose waves rolled to and fro through our churches for seven years, and on the full tide of which Whitefield preached.

So much for the place of this little company of morning worshipers in the political and religious history of our land. As to their material and social circumstances, they were for the most part plain farmers, who themselves or their fathers, toward the close of the previous century, or about fifty years before, had begun to occupy lands in what is now the town of Meriden. For such families as lay in the southern half of our town, the church at Wallingford had been the nearest place of worship. The way was long, the roads miserable, so that, with the increase of settlements in this section, a separate place of worship became a necessity. In 1724, "the north farmers," i. e. those in this section, which was then within the limits of Wallingford, were permitted by special vote in Wallingford town meeting, to "hire a minister for four months this winter on their own charge." Thus one hundred and fifty-two years ago our fathers held their first regular preaching services. In the following year, 1725, they formed themselves into a separate ecclesiastical society under the name of Meriden. For two years more they maintained preaching only in the winter, and that in private houses. In summer they could go down to Wallingford. In 1727 this little church on the hill was built. So lately as the twenty-second of this present month of October, 1729, these worshipers had now, at length, organized themselves into a Christian church on a day specially set apart as a day of fasting and prayer.

Thus slowly, step by step,—thus wearily and with sacrifice,—thus earnestly and devoutly, did our fathers plant themselves here as a Christian community, the center of which was evermore to be the Christian church. They were the men who had cleared away the forests for the first cultivated farms, and they were clearing them still. Selecting what seemed to them the most promising sites for future homes, they had built and were still building their houses in what was only fifty years before a wilderness, lying dangerously remote, on account of Indian wars, from the settlements at Wallingford on the one side and Hartford on the other.

The surroundings of the little meeting-house were still wild. It was perched up there on the hill far away from any of the centers into which our fathers of Meriden had settled. Looking down from it the eye swept a large territory in every direction, which was then without a village, and must have been mostly covered with forests, through which rough roads led to distant and widely separated clusters of farm-houses. Broad Street was probably at that time without a house. Over all of what we call the older part of Meriden, thickly crowded now with dwellings, stores, public buildings, and manufactories, there was nothing to mark the site of the future city. To the east, around those swampy lands which lie south of the Middletown road, half way between us and the mountains, lay a little settlement, which, taking its name from the swamp, was called "Dogs' Misery," to note the fact that in those dense thickets, wild animals, taking refuge, were able to baffle the dogs of hunters in their pursuit, or turned upon them when driven to bay and tore them to death.

Far away to the north, on the Old Colony road, a number of farmers had settled, beyond the present glass works, up as far as the Old Stone House which first bore the name of Meriden. In that section there were people enough to make an important move. Fourteen persons signed a petition, which, touching so large a matter, had to be addressed " To the Honorable, the Governor and Council and house of representatives, in General Cort assembled, in his Majesties colony of Connecticut, att New Haven, 8th of October, 1724." The people represent that they " are compelled to drive unruly cattell nere 6 or 9 miles " before they can find a pound. They pray " that there may be order for a pound near ye Meriden or Stone House," and for this they solemnly aver that they will "ever pray." It is to be hoped they got the pound. To the southwest also there was a settlement, at Hanover, which had been laid out into village lots as early as 1689. Down in the valley at the Corner, or in what was then called Pilgrims' Harbor, there was also the beginning of a settlement.

The distribution of these little groups of farmers at remote quarters of the town, had made the question of the location of the first meeting-house one of great difficulty. Discussion ran high,—the interests of the several sections were hard to adjust. But, strangely enough, as it seems to us, in view of the present distribution of population, neither the Corner, nor yet Hanover, nor the farmers of the north, were strong enough to overrule the then thriving community of "Dogs' Misery." It won the day. The Center had no existence and was not taken into the account. The timbers were gathered on the southwestern slope of the hill; but those who contended for a more westerly location brought their teams in the night, and, with something of Yankee fun and grit mixed with the work, dragged the timbers over the little brook, which still runs at the western foot of Meeting-house Hill, to a point near the Avery Hall place on Curtiss street. They showed their grit and they had their fun; but the very men and teams which had sweated at the work through the night, had to sweat the next day over the work of drawing the timbers back again. We do not learn that any feud was perpetuated from this discussion.

The little congregation worshiped, and grew in the humble church, during twenty-eight years, from the time of its building. There, without fires in the cold winters, and through long services, the good women sat patiently wrapped in furs and mufflers, while the men stamped their feet to keep them warm. To have heated a church would have been a desecrating luxury. It would have been a soft piety that could not endure any and all degrees of temperature in the house of God. So the wind swept over the little building, and the snow piled its drifts around it until the spring came with its first robin song, and the good people basked in the sun again, before the door. Then the summer flung out its leaves over the forest, and October turned them to crimson and yellow and brown again, and the autumnal ingathering of fruit

2

closed with its Thanksgiving feast, in the scattered farm-houses, where broad-mouthed fire places, piled high with logs, filled the kitchens and parlors with light that shone out through the windows into the night, while the flames roared and crackled up the chimney throat, and apples, and cider, and nuts, and country games went round, until the tallow-dipped candles burned low in the sockets of the candlesticks, and the ashes were raked over the still glimmering heaps of coals to keep the fire till morning.

The number of those who were first joined in the covenant of the church was fifty-one, of whom twenty-one were men and thirty were women.

The names which appear in this list are for the most part names which have been and still are identified with the history of the town—the names of your fathers—the Royces, the Yales, the Merriams, the Fosters, Collins, and Hough, and Ives, and Way, and Curtiss, and Camp. The number of families in the place in 1724, five years before the organization of the church, were only thirty-five, and it had probably not much increased in 1729. As you have seen that those thirty-five families were divided between some four different sections of the town, there could have been nothing really approaching the pretentions of a village, throughout the present area of Meriden.

The little church grew. Mr. Perkins, whose historical sketch, prepared with great care, and published in 1849, will always be the starting point for the study of our history, says that so far as he can learn, for "year after year, not more than one or two were united to the church annually." But in this he is mistaken.

The record shows that in 1730, twenty-seven were received, and in 1731, at least eight, and though the record is confused at this point, perhaps nineteen were received in the latter year. During the thirty-six years following the organization of the church, two hundred and fifty-three persons were added to the list of the original membership. This is an addition of seven a year, as an average for the whole period. It seems that the little church, in common with many others in New England, felt the great wave of revival in the times of Edwards and Whitefield; for I find in the year 1741, after Whitefield had preached in the fall of 1740, on the steps, thirty-one were united to the church.

But we dare not leave out of the account of this rapid growth, the severe and strong labors of that first pastor of the church, whom we shall find, if we go back to that October service, at which we began our history; standing in the first month of his settlement, small of stature, a youth of twenty-one years, to whom it is to be given to see a strong church rise out of these small beginnings, whose work it is to be, touched by the Spirit of God and of liberty, to lead this young flock out of the wilderness and through the storm into a larger place.

Theophilus Hall was a man of powerful intellect, and of large heart. As I have searched among old papers, it has been an inspiration to come into contact with the earnestness, and the vigor of this man, who began to preach a hundred and fifty years ago. If you picture your early fathers, dear friends, as sitting in listless attitudes, dozing through long discourses—

up there on the hill—you are wide of the mark. The uninteresting preacher, if you have ever had him, was of later date. This man's words flashed; his short, quick, clean cut sentences went to the mark. His familiar style with its "don't," and "won't," and "can't," and its "you'll," makes it easy to listen, while his sentiments belong more to a future age than to the one in which he speaks. Apt illustrations and sudden surprises give zest to the flow of his thought. He is direct, personal, and eloquent. I do not hesitate to say, that if he stood in one of our pulpits to-day, he would stand there as a thoroughly popular preacher, whom men would love to hear preach, and would love to criticise when he should be through preaching. He knew no fetters. He believed in religious liberty as distinguished from ecclesiastical bonds and oppressions; he believed in civil liberty and was bold to speak it; he believed in liberty of thought; and he believed and did not fear to preach that doctrine of love which goes down into the heart of the practical christian life—a life like Christ's. Of those who *talk* much of religion, but know little of the practical part he cries—" Such are they that are making the religion of Jesus Christ to consist only in a heated imagination, in trances, visions, and enthusiastic flights and raptures; that are affecting *party names and terms* valuing themselves thereon, imposing their own sentiments upon others, and stigmatizing those that can't conform to them or pronounce their darling Shibboleths." "No better are they that are casting a slight upon holiness and sanctity, good works and obedience to the commands of Christ as absolutely necessary terms—prerequisite to our acceptance with God. Such *talk* as this, is it not against the crown and dignity of heaven?" To those who cry against works and preach a passive faith, he answers: "Is not believing as much doing and acting as any other duty? . . . . . I know not why the word (works) is restricted to bodily exercise . . . . . The love of God and repentance of sin are as much works and acts of obedience as any external duty whatsoever. And is not faith the same?

"Saving faith is the submission of the whole man to Jesus Christ as our Lord and Master."

And here are things, touching the subject of faith, I have wished to say and have never dared to say them. *He said* them more than a hundred years ago. "There are those," says he, "who have a hope in God, and if you'll inquire into the reason of it they'll boldly tell you, 'We know we are sinners, but Christ has died to save such; there is merit enough in Him; He is a whole Saviour; and our whole dependence is on the righteousness and merits of Jesus Christ.'" Then turning to his hearers, he cries: "but you'll say, 'all this is nothing but presumption, a *false* hope and trust.'" "I know it well enough," he answers; "but all hope and trust in God will be no better if there is nothing else." Bold words, dear friends, but true. Then, addressing himself to one who asks: "Is not this a legal way of justification?" he cries: "I answer, legal or illegal, it matters not, if it be the way the Gospel establishes and Christ and His apostles preached."

Do you wish for more? "A principle of obedi-

2*

ence, a divine conformity, is absolutely necessary to acceptance with God. Can it possibly be otherwise? Are there any contraries in Nature greater than sin and holiness? Can a swinish nature, whose whole delight is in the filth of sin, relish the pure joys of heaven?"

His plainness, and his great liberality, and his eloquence, all come out in the sermon on the death of Rev. Isaac Stiles, of North Haven, preached June 1st, 1760. In speaking of the righteous, he says: "What great blessings to the world such are. All men are not blessings to the world; some are the foremost judgments and the greatest plagues on the earth. Their lives are prolonged in judgment, and it is a mercy to the world when they are taken out of it." Then, after illustrating, he goes on: " But, O, 'tis good men—not such as wear religion only as a cloak to cover their deformities; or make use of it as an engine of cruelty, or a handle to serve vile purposes; nor every party zealot that thinks himself holier than others, is for calling fire from heaven upon all that differ from him ;—but *right down honest, upright* men, that are the greatest blessings under heaven....These are the gems and pearls of the earth." And in the same sermon, this burst of eloquence on death: "What joy to leave the stormy ocean and enter into port! To come off from the field of battle with trophies of victory! Much greater, yea, joy unspeakable and full of glory, to leave all the troubles of this world for peace and joy in the heavenly! Blessed soul, that exchanges corruption for incorruption; this crazy body for one furnished like Christ's glorious body; and this mortal life for a crown of glory that fadeth not away! ' O, death, where is thy sting !' "

Great soul! No wonder the people loved him ; no wonder the church grew ; no wonder in 1755 the house was too small ; and, after twenty-eight years, they built the preacher a larger church, near where this one now stands,—a church which weathered the storms of the Revolution, and looked down on the changes of Meriden life and population for seventy-six years. No wonder, too, that one who spoke so well, but so keenly, found his share of enemies, and criticisms, and pastoral trials. No matter how conciliatory his course, no matter how tenderly he spoke,—and his words were sometimes like the words of a lover,— there were those who would gladly have thwarted him in his efforts. When Dr. Dana, pastor of the mother church in Wallingford, was put under the ban of the consociation, and a bitter attempt was made to throw him out of his pulpit, on the charge of heretical doctrine, the pastor of this church stood by him and invited him to his pulpit. For this act of liberty, as well as, it would seem, out of opposition to the sentiments of the pastor, an attempt was made to call Mr. Hall to account before the association of the county. I find on the record an entry of a very full church meeting on the 24th day of May, 1762, to the effect that, "after solemn prayer and supplication made to Almighty God, the complaint against the pastor of this church, given to the association of New Haven County, and signed by Ebenezer Prindle, Gideon Ives junior and Noah Yale, was laid before the church."

It seems probable that the complaint before the association urged against Mr. Hall heretical interpretations of the gospel and the crime of exchanging with his neighbor of the Wallingford church. The Meriden church met the case promptly, stood by its pastor, declared in the " most unanimous manner " that the complainants had, for a great number of years past, appeared uneasy and dissatisfied with the preaching of the word ; had been wont to take it up in a sense contrary to the acceptation of the people in general ; that there was no just ground for their complaint ; that it seemed designed to disturb the peace and quiet of the church ; and that the preaching of Mr. Dana was acceptable and agreeable. Thus flatly did the church rebuke the men who looked for an occasion to break the strength of the pastor. The church went before the association and the affair seems to have been dropped.

The records of this period are very scanty, and are much taken up with matters of discipline, which in our earlier history was more faithfully administered than now, and took cognizance of matters such as we should be very likely to pass by. Lest some here might possibly be nearly enough related to the persons concerned in one curious case of discipline to be disturbed at the mention of their full names, I will only say, that in the year 1745 there was a complaint against certain members whose Christian names were, Enos, Benjamin, John, Samuel, Noah, David, and another David, who were all suspended on account of disorders committed in the night time. The case of these persons, bearing a remarkable array of scripture names, came under the cognizance of the civil courts and judgment was pronounced against them. From the church record, and from a curious old paper which has come into my hands through one of the families of the parish, but which had never been understood until the correspondence between it and the church record was discovered, it appears that Enos and Benjamin and John and Samuel and Noah and the two Davids had been guilty of making night hideous "by ringing bells and blowing horns on the highway." The neighborhood took offense at it. It is possible there was some political bearing to their action, though it may have been only one of those frolics which were liable to be treated as breaches of the peace. They were convicted in court, and the church record quaintly says, that Enos and Noah and one of the Davids, before the church, acknowledged that said actions were neither justifiable nor commendable, and they were really sorry that they had any hand in it and promised that they would do so no more. The church took them back, but Benjamin, Samuel, and the other David, justified their conduct, and their case was sent up to the association, from which august body it came back with advice to the church to receive them if they would " promise to behave orderly for the time to come," otherwise to hold them under suspension. The church followed the advice, but I have not yet learned whether the three obstinate ones ever gave in.

How hard it was for the pastor to adjust all the affairs of the young but growing church, appears from the course of some of the people in connection

with the erection of a new meeting-house. It took
five years to discuss the location of that building.
Mr. Hall was evidently a man of affairs, and was the
owner of a very considerable property. He lived on
the spot where his direct descendant, Mr. Avery
Hall, now lives, in a house of which the present one
is said to be as nearly as possible a copy. He built
also, for his son, the large house over the way from
us, on the corner of Broad and Main streets, long
used for a hotel ; and he gave the acre of ground on
which we stand for the erection of the new church.
But there was jealousy of the pastor's influence.
Some evidently thought it would not do to build on
ground owned by the minister. Some advantage
might accrue to him. The acceptance of the gift
might bring him some larger claim upon the people,
and increase his power. A party sprang up in opposition, but the day was again carried against the
opposition. Thus pestered and troubled, you will not
wonder that the great heart of Theophilus Hall grew
weary, and that, in an ordination sermon preached at
Berwick, (Matthew Merriam's ordination, Sept. 25,
1765,) only less than two years before he died, he
should have poured out his soul in words like these,
on the trials and the joys of a pastor's life: " With
respect to the people, innumerable difficulties arise
from this matter ; there is so much weakness and
ignorance, so much pride and self-conceit among
them, so many different tastes and opinions, and
their state and circumstances so very various, that it
is almost impossible rightly to divide the word of
truth among them. If you conform to one, you may

be sure you will offend another; and if you preach the truth, it may be you will displease them all.... Some are too knowing to be taught, others too proud to be reproved, and how many are there disposed to find fault? They look upon their ministers with a jealous eye, and are apt to think the least failing in them an unpardonable crime.

"How often is this the case, that one or the other of these dilemmas or the like are retorted upon us by the people? If we take no care of our secular interest, we are idle and indolent men. If we preach anything new to them, 'it is heresy;' but if we don't, then we are charged with old sermons. If we are familiar with our people, they will despise us; but if we keep them at a proper distance, then we lord it over God's heritage. 'John came neither eating nor drinking, and they say he hath a devil. The Son of Man came eating and drinking, and they say, Behold a man gluttonous and a wine bibber, a friend of publicans and sinners.' "

Alas! dear friends, that thirty odd years with a single people should have forced such a passage from such a man. And yet the dear little church had stood by him until it had grown with him into strength. From a membership of fifty it had risen to be a strong church.* From the little meeting-house on the hill the congregation had removed to a new and substantial house in the future center of the growing population.

The hard struggle of the day of small things was

---

* In 1770 the membership was 185 and the familes in the parish 123.

over. The voice which for thirty-seven years had sounded a ringing note of liberty, and had fearlessly proclaimed the need among men of a divine life, is at last hushed. The first pastor is dead. In the early spring of 1767, they bore him through the scenes of his toil, over the little brook, up the steep hill-side, past the site of the little church, to the burying-ground on yonder southern slope. There they laid him down and covered him with the sod, and on the red sandstone slab over his grave they wrote these words:

IN MEMORY

OF

THEOPHILUS HALL,

Pastor of the church, who, having for thirty-seven years discharged the duties of his function with distinguished fidelity and accomplished Christian life, the uniform disciple of Jesus Christ,

DECEASED MARCH 23D, 1767, IN THE SIXTIETH YEAR OF HIS AGE.

" They that be wise shall shine as the brightness of the firmament."

We need no account of that funeral. Over that grave all contention was hushed. In it all bitterness was buried. Love wove around it a garland of memories brought from all their rural homes, and the benediction of God's peace was upon it. For more than a hundred years the grass has freshened and faded over it; for more than a hundred years the winter wind has swept it and the summer rains have moistened it. To-day the slab which commemorates that life of our early history lies neglected and broken on the ground, desecrated by the sport of heedless passers-by. But the lives that were made better by that life, the tears that were dried, and the mourning hearts that were comforted, and the wayward ones that were saved by it, are praising it still and will praise it for ever. How mightily that life and that vigorous thought have influenced the growing future of this place, even down to the present generation, we know not. But I am proud, dear friends, to have been instrumental, this day, in bringing the memory of it out of the forgetfulness of the past and re-consecrating it in the heart of this genetion.

3

SECOND CENTENNIAL SERMON

PREACHED ON THE

ONE HUNDRED AND FORTY-SEVENTH ANNIVERSARY

OF THE ORGANIZATION OF THE

CONGREGATIONAL CHURCH

IN MERIDEN.

SUNDAY, OCTOBER 22D, 1876.

——— - ...

TEXT—REV. 3: 8.—"Behold, I have set before thee an open door, and no man can shut it."

SERMON.

Once more, my friends, let us try to get a picture
of the popular life to which our church, by God's help,
about the year 1770, was still supplying moral and
spiritual power. The church is nothing without the
people. The kingdom of heaven comes to society
busied with schemes of national development and of
political government. On this troubled sea of human
interests, with its clashing waves, the church of God
may seem only a driven boat, with quivering mast and
storm-reefed sail, tossed at the mercy of innumerable
waves ; but through the storm and under the cloud
she is God's pilot-boat to individuals and nations.

Over what kind of seas is our little church, at the
time of the death of its first pastor, helping to guide
the people? There have been great changes since
that 22d of October, of the year 1729, when, on a day
set apart for fasting and prayer, your fathers entered
into the covenant of a Christian church. Thirty-
eight years have passed, during which the nation and
the parish with it have been growing rapidly in numbers and in material wealth. The last two or three
years of the life of Hall had also been spent among
scenes of political excitement, under which the nerve
of the nation first quivered and then strung itself for
battle. The lenient policy of King George the Second

3*

had been succeeded by the oppressive policy of the mad King George the Third. Taxation by sea was to be followed by taxation on American soil, which our fathers declared subversive of American liberties. It is an old story, but these Centennial sermons would be tame without it. It was God's narrow way to the open door. On the 27th of February, 1765, British legislation for the Colonies brought the stamp act through the House of Commons. On the eighth of March following, the House of Lords agreed to it without " amendment, debate, protest, division, or single dissentient vote," and George the Third signed it on the 22d day of March, just two years and one day before the death of that " zealous advocate for civil and religious liberty," Meriden's first pastor ; who, therefore, lived long enough to witness the recoil of a stunned nation at the reception of the news of that act, and to see the rebound as the nation sprang to the work of resistance. He heard often, no doubt, the cry of " Liberty, Property, and No stamps," which rang on the streets even in the mouths of children. He was a sharer in the excitement here in Connecticut, when those five hundred farmers and freeholders, mounted on horseback, armed with freshly peeled white cudgels, forced the stamp officer, Ingersoll, on the broad Wethersfield street, to resign his office, throw up his hat, and three times shout, " Liberty and Property."

What part our Meriden fathers took in all this, we have little left on record to tell us ; but we know that the great tide wave did not pass over these hills and through these valleys without gathering force as it swept by our ancestral homes, and the doors of the new church on Meriden green. We know that when, in January, 1766, the Sons of Liberty, of New York, sent out their proclamation declaring that they would go to the last extremity, and venture their lives and fortunes, effectually to prevent the stamp act, their resolution was speedily brought to Connecticut, and the town of Wallingford, of which this Meriden parish then formed a part, in a meeting in which, no doubt, the Meriden pastor and people participated, voted a fine of twenty shillings on any inhabitant "that should use or improve any stamped velum or paper ;" and the organization of Sons of Liberty formed in the town of Wallingford and Meriden declared, with their brethren of New York, that they were prepared " to oppose the unconstitutional stamp act, to the last extremity, even to take the field." It would be a precious memorial of those brave spirits who nursed the fire which, ten years later, flamed out in the Declaration of Independence, if I were able here to produce some of the words which fell from the pulpit on the Sundays which followed those stirring weeks down to the time when Parliament, one year before Mr. Hall's death, repealed that act. He who could speak so eloquently and boldly must have spoken most eloquently and boldly in those last days, from which he was so soon to enter into rest. But I find no word of it all. In the lull which followed the intense excitement of that first great struggle of the people, he passed away, and left the church to plunge into a contest with the ecclesiastical powers around it, wherein our fathers showed that ecclesiastical freedom was not less precious to them than civil liberty.

That controversy over the installation of the Rev. John Hubbard, the second pastor of this church, has gone into history, along with the celebrated controversy in Wallingford over the ordination of Dr. Dana. It was more than a controversy between a majority and a minority in a country church. It was a contest between the rights of the local church under the congregational system, and associations and consociations ruling over the churches with authority. It was a continuation of the struggle, in these Connecticut churches, between Congregationalism pure and simple and a Presbyterianized Congregationalism set forth by the Saybrook Platform (in the year 1708,) and established by act of the General Assembly of these Connecticut colonies as the basis of a *quasi* State church. The roots of the Hubbard controversy strike deep into religious liberty. Things were ripe here, as you know from my first discourse, for the breaking out of an already disaffected party, when, in the October* following the death of Theophilus Hall, the church invited John Hubbard, of New Haven, then about forty years of age, to preach for four weeks on probation. The appearance of that preacher on the scene was the signal for action. Mr. Hubbard was reputed, as reputation then went, to be unsound. He could not have preached more than one Sunday, when† forty-seven members of the society petitioned their fellow-members to advise with either association

---

of New Haven County, as was then the custom, on the subject of a candidate for the pastoral office. But the church was shy of associational interference. It meant to choose its own pastor.

On the 2d of November, having probably heard the eight probationary sermons, it voted, forty-two to twenty-one, in favor of inviting Mr. Hubbard "to the pastoral office." The minority appealed to the association. The association summoned the accused pastor-elect before it ; the pastor-elect denied the jurisdiction of that ecclesiastical court, and the association replied by taking away his license. The consociation with its higher authority confirmed this act. So John Hubbard preached without a license.

The church entered on its record a declaration made* "by a full vote," the preamble of which throws light on the state of things among the churches at that time. "Whereas," it says, "there has much controversy and dispute existed in this Colony of late concerning ecclesiastical discipline, and particularly concerning the authority of councils and the rights of particular churches, we think it expedient to declare explicitly our purpose to 'stand fast in the liberty wherewith Christ hath made us free.'" "We understand," the declaration goes on to say, "that no consociation has right, by the constitution, to take cognizance of or intermeddle with any of the affairs or doings of any particular church upon the desire or application of private members of said church, unless said church first consented thereto or had excom-

---

*November 20th, 1767.

municated said private members. . . . . We declare ourselves to be a *Congregational* church, and we understand the constitution as allowing and securing to us the full enjoyment of the rights of Congregational churches, especially the right of exercising discipline by ourselves and choosing our own pastor."

People had got into a troublesome way of talking about rights in those days, of British navigation laws and stamp acts. The Wallingford matter, too, had put these men on their guard. They held to the value of Congregationalism as a system of church liberty. Their dead pastor had taught them that. They believed in the rule of majorities ; and they had heard in the last thirty-seven years too free a discussion of Christian doctrine to be alarmed by the cry of heresy. That declaration, flung out on the 20th of November, was a warning to the consociation, which was already on the move.

On the 29th of December, the month following that declaration, the parish of Meriden was the scene of lively discussion in every family, at the early morning meal, and by every fireside in the evening. On that day a council of churches met at the call of the majority to ordain John Hubbard ; and, on the same day, the Consociation of New Haven County met also, here in Meriden, to prevent the ordination. For four days these two ecclesiastical bodies held sessions, discussed, resolved, remonstrated, and grew warm over against each other, until at last the council which the majority had called "considered the broken state of the society," and were of opinion it was not best to proceed to ordination. But the trouble was not over.

In the following March,* in a protest which sounds very much like 1776, our church re-asserted its privileges. That document, which sets forth its grievances and declares its withdrawal from the consociation, is worthy of a full reading here were there time for it. It begins by pointing to the relation of this trouble to that in Wallingford ; refers to the interference of the consociation at the time when the council met in Meriden ; declares it does not know what is further intended, but supposes that unless the church desist from its choice of a pastor, it is to be treated as the Wallingford church was—the minority to be declared the church, and they themselves scattered "as the ashes of the martyrs in the air, and their bones at the grave's mouth." They declare that they see no safety but in flight. They therefore renounce the consociation, and assert that they will pay no regard to its authority. Then within a week† they offer to the minority to give up their preference for Mr. Hubbard, "though his preaching and labors are very agreeable to us," provided the opposers of Mr. Hubbard's settlement "join with the major part of this church in asserting and maintaining that Christian liberty which we so highly esteem, ... renounce the consociation . . . . until said consociation gives up their unwarrantable claims." The entry of the scribe, Benjamin Rice, at the close of this proposition shows how things were going : "The above proposal was universally assented to by the major part and it was wholly rejected by the minor with contempt."

* March 22d, 1768.   † March 28th.

The minority persevered and carried the case before the Colonial Assembly.*   The majority in its turn called a second council having two ministers from this Colony of Connecticut, one of whom was the Rev. James Dana, (who was also scribe of the council,) and four from outside the colony.   Of these, the Rev. Dr. Ezra Styles, of Newport, afterwards President of Yale College, was brother-in-law of Mr. Hubbard.   The others were the Rev. Joseph Lothrop, of Springfield, Rev. Robert Buck, also of Springfield, and the Rev. John Ballentine.   This council met on the 20th day of that always lovely month of June (1769).   Before it appeared a committee of the association on behalf of the minority, and before it also appeared the minority itself, with a protest.   The discussion continued with protest, propositions, and rejections, until the majority of the church—declaring that they do not believe the difficulties can ever be adjusted, and that they have exhausted all expedients—close with an expressed conviction that if, as had been proposed, a mutual council agreed on by the parties in the church should meet and advise Mr. Hubbard not to settle, even that would not bring peace ; but on the contrary, " we never shall be as well united as now, but fear our unhappy dispute will terminate in the great interest of the Church of England."   How far that last dark hint about the formation of an Episcopal Church in the parish of Meriden may have influenced the minds of the reverend ministers on that council, we can only guess.   But the council was convinced,

*May, 1768.

and on the 22d of June, granted the petition of the church, and ordained the pastor of its choice. Both sides in the controversy had shown the persevering spirit of the times.

What the views of Mr. Hubbard were, I have not as yet been able to ascertain;[*] but from such hints as I am able to gather, nothing in his theology would render him objectionable to any church of ordinary intelligence at the present day. The contest was due to the progress of thought in a time when men's minds were thoroughly roused—when there was a great tendency to free discussions, and when with the chafing at political bondage there came a new and fresh assertion of the liberty of the old Congregational way against the restraints of a half way Presbyterian-ism. Such times would necessarily involve conflict.

The discussion continued in the colony after the council had decided the case. A portion of the church withdrew and maintained separate worship. But the magnetism of men is often mightier than the preju-dices of men. The fine qualities of the new pastor forced themselves upon the hearts of the opposers ; his kindness, his charity, and his courtesy won them all back. Animated and interesting as a preacher, his freedom of thought possessed a charm for that age of liberty, and his "unusually pleasant and benignant countenance," remembered still in 1848 by the sur-vivors of his ministry, disarmed malice, if malice there was, or dissipated innocent but unnecessary fears. Moreover, the time when he entered upon his minis-

---

[*] For Mr. Hubbard's Confession of Faith, since discovered, see Appendix.

try was auspicious. It was a time pregnant with that future, in which men's thoughts turned from the smaller strifes of parishes to the concerns of a nation passing through the baptism of blood. The years were speeding rapidly on to the revolution, with its sacrifices, its homes mourning over the slain, and its long watching for the fulfillment of patriotic hopes. These years were favorable for such a man to win the hearts of the people.

It is a significant fact which comes to my knowledge just at the moment of writing these lines, that perhaps the only person living, who was born in Meriden during Mr. Hubbard's ministry, an old lady, residing near Aurora, Illinois, a hundred years of age this fall, very naively said to a great-grandson of our John Hubbard, that her father's family found it convenient to remove from Meriden while she was very young. As she was born in 1776, and circumstances point to the tory leanings of her father, it will readily be understood *how* convenient it was for the family to take its departure.

Mr. Hubbard lived to see the close of that war and to share in the rejoicings over a victorious peace. But at about this time he was thrown from his sleigh and so severely injured that he ceased preaching. He lingered among an affectionate people some three years longer, when he died and was buried, under the chill winds of a November day, in the new cemetery beneath the trees to the south of us, the land of which he himself had deeded to the town of Meriden. There, at the head of one of the graves, those who revere the past may find a quaint old free-stone slab on which his people thus delicately commemorated his virtues:

IN MEMORY

OF THE

REV. JOHN HUBBARD, A. M.,

Pastor of the Church in Meriden, who

DIED NOV. 18TH, 1776, ÆTAT 60.

He was a rational and serious Christian, exemplary
for gravity, integrity, piety and benevolence. He
was an able minister of the New Testament and
beloved by all his flock for his faithfulness
and apostolic diligence in the work of the
ministry, and for the prudence, kindness, and humanity which adorned
his manners and rendered him a
most excellent pastor."

By the side of that weather-worn slab of sandstone stands another, which commemorates his wife,
Mary, who died March 2, 1806, having that day
completed her 70th year. Of her the sculptor's
chisel says: "An early Christian profession was
adorned by her living to Christ. With a rare tender-
ness of conscience, she kept in view the glory of God
in all the duties of her relations and conditions. Re-
marking the Providence which numbereth the hairs
of our heads, she improved by every incident." Then,
with a touch of sympathy, the chisel tenderly adds :
"The comforts of vital piety, which she sensibly enjoyed, were subject to intervals of extreme mental
darkness." "Light is sown for the righteous."

If I were to search for some words with which to

close this notice of a charitable life, I could hardly find any more worthy of our heeding, as members of a Christian church and as neighbors and friends, than these, taken from the only sermon of Mr. Hubbard's which has come into my hands. It is a pungent but kindly one on the sin of backbiting, preached March 12th, 1776, a hundred years ago. After defining that vice as consisting "in speaking ill of others, slandering and reproaching of them in their absence, and consequently when they have no opportunity to exculpate or vindicate themselves," and after saying that "Besides the unreasonableness of this practice, it is a mean vice, having its special deformity as it betrayeth a soul that is either wholly devoid of every principle of ingenuity and friendship, or inattentive to the great and sacred law of love and charity," he closes by making this application: "The subject remindeth us also of the importance of cultivating a spirit of universal candor, charity, and love. . . . . Then shall we be disposed to put on, as the elect of God, bowels of mercies, kindness, humbleness of mind; then will the God of love and peace dwell among us."

Before the death of John Hubbard, the Rev. John Willard had been settled as colleague pastor in June, 1786. I am able to add almost nothing to what others have written in regard to him and his pastorate. His work here fell in that unfortunate period of financial depression and moral deterioration which follows upon long and exhausting wars. It is not likely that the population increased rapidly. He was an animated preacher, of very tall and slender figure, and a sermon which has come into my hands, preached in a neighboring parish, on the training of children, was by request, I believe, of that parish, put into print.

On his settlement, the old division in the church showed itself afresh, and he seems to have had a troubled ministry. Again the doctrinal discussion was renewed as under Hubbard. It is a fact, having a bearing no doubt on his work, that the First Baptist church in Meriden was organized in the midst of that controversy, two months after his settlement, and the Episcopal church was organized before the close of his ministry. It is said that great numbers either deserted public worship altogether or transferred themselves to other denominations. The old yeast of discontent was doing its work. The history of the previous twenty years, the progress and diversity of opinion in the church, the conflict between the new and the old, had made a rendering of old church ties inevitable, and these denominations offered the occasion for a result which was already being precipitated. Discouraged by causes which were, no doubt, beyond human control, Mr. Willard committed what, I fear, was the error of resigning his post, and was dismissed in 1802. By that event, for the first time the pastoral relation in this church was violently broken, and, since that day, no pastor has rounded out the work of his whole life among you. One has come back to die after an absence of years, and another has been brought here and buried; but pastorates have been increasingly brief, and no pastor has died in the harness. Has it always been the preacher's fault?

I learn* that in the ten years ending in 1795, all of

---

* Manuscript sermon of Mr. Hinsdale.

4*

which fell in Mr. Willard's ministry, the number of additions to the church were sixty-five or an average of six and one-half per year.

We must not leave the last century, my friends, without a glimpse at the state of society in that period which we love to think of as the romantic period of American history. In the last quarter of the last century, the drift of population pointed more and more towards the formation of an important center along the line of our present Broad street. Here the church had been built; here, across the way, the house which afterwards became the half-way tavern for the days of stages, had been built; on the hill, where Edward Miller's house now stands, the Rev. John Hubbard built and lived in a house which has since been removed to the east side of South Broad street, and is occupied by our friend, Mr. Sanderson. The highway which forms the present street in front of the church had been laid out, and farther north, at the head of what is now Liberty street, Mr. Willard, the third pastor, built what, for the time, was a sufficiently stately house, the same square-roofed building, with projecting upper story, which has been since removed to a point on Broad street, opposite Mr. Bassett's. The place of burial, too, had been changed from the sunny hill-side to the cemetery just south of us. These private houses with the church, ranging along the wide but rough highway, already formed a center towards which the population drifted, until the opening of the railroad.

The spirit of progress and change was working out

the greater future of Meriden and the whole land. The survivors of those subjects of the British king, who first gathered in the church built on this spot, had now become free citizens of a free country. The colony of Connecticut had become a State. He that "openeth and no man shutteth, and shutteth and no man openeth," had set before them an open door.

The people who came into church on those Sundays in the latter portion of the last century, were men and women of deep convictions, of heroic courage, of mighty endurance, and of earnest life. They were earnest, but not so grave, I imagine, as some of us have pictured them. The stir of those days was favorable to vivacity of manners, and the Yankee loved a strain of wit then as well as now. In society there was a certain courtliness which we have dropped. The dress was more pretentious, or seems more so to us. The short clothes, with long hose, buckles at the knees, and buckled shoes, the cocked hats and full white or gray wigs, which were worn in public, give an air of stateliness to our fathers, but they did not forget to be playful. Their homes were plain but cheerful, with the opening fields around them in summer and with the blazing wood fires in winter. Luxuries had not found their way into domestic life. The women did house-work. The oppression of trade by England had stimulated home industry. Spinning-wheels for wool and flax hummed lullabys to children in the broad kitchens, and hand-looms clattered through the winter days as they wove the yarn or the thread into homespun. The homes of ministers were not always sober. Doctor Styles, the same that formed one of the council which ordained John Hubbard, tells us in his manuscript diary at Yale College, of a donation party at his house in Newport, where the women had a spinning match, at which there were thirty-seven spinning-wheels going at one time.

There was a grand break down of denominational lines, at least, that day. Among the spinners were two Quakers, six Baptists, and twenty-nine of his own society. Besides the spinners were sixteen reelers to reel the yarn. Sixty persons dined at the parsonage. What a humming and buzzing! Do you suppose those fifty and more women made no music at the pastor's house? The fathers and mothers of '76 were earnest but not over-staid people. They were progressive folks. The world moved fast in the last quarter of the last century.

In the houses there were no carpets. Even in 1802, there was but one in the town. Down to the year 1789 there had never been owned here any thing more nearly approaching a pleasure wagon or traveling buggy, than the three two-wheeled rude chaises without top, which had hitherto constituted the turnout of the town. People—men and women, young and old—rode on horseback from house to house. I have heard my mother, who was born in 1800, tell of the merry times, when young men came to take young ladies to ride behind them on pillions, and dashed away two upon a horse over Torringford hills. Women, as well as men, were good riders in those days. In a country where there were only rough roads, every body learned to mount a horse.

Mr. Perkins tells us that down to the year 1802, there was not here a single road that was rounded up as we make roads now. When the Hartford and New Haven Turnpike through the center of the town was completed, about the year 1800, it was considered a " vast, wonderful, and curious work." People came to see it, just as they afterwards flocked to see the first railroad. The completion of such roads was a necessary preliminary to those splendid stage lines which, down to 1830 or '40, furnished the swiftest mode of communication, with their relays, and their proud drivers on rattling coaches, shaking the reins over four running horses, ringing out the signal note of the French horn, then seizing the long whip and sending the cracking lash around the ears of the leaders, as coach, passengers, baggage, and mail rolled down past the village houses towards the half-way house on the corner.

The morals of the last portion of the last century in this town of Meriden, may be gathered from the style of church discipline and from the well-known drinking habits of society. The population of Meriden in 1790 is said not to have been more than about nine hundred, and for that population, and down to 1812, there were not less than five and perhaps eight taverns, all keeping liquors. But it must be remembered that the traveling habits of the public, in a time when journeys were made on horseback, and later in wagons and stages, made taverns necessary in a place so favorably situated as Meriden was for a resting point on the great thoroughfare from Springfield and Hartford through New Haven to New York.

But the old tavern with its bar, its great room for strangers lounging before the open fire, its numbers of all classes brought together for a night away from home, with its practice of social drinking which then pervaded society, with its story-telling, and its village lounging—that being the place to which people naturally resorted to hear the news from strangers, and often the place for distribution of the mails—the old New England tavern of the last century and the early part of this was not a promoter of what we should term good morals.

Slavery existed in a mild form among our fathers of the last century. In the year 1790, Connecticut had two thousand seven hundred and fifty-nine slaves ; and even down to the year 1840, in this State the process of gradual emancipation which had been adopted here had still left us seventeen slaves. Mr. Perkins estimates that in 1770, there were in the whole town of Wallingford and Meriden fifty-six slaves—an estimate based upon the records of deaths for thirty-eight years. The hardships of slavery, bitter enough in any case, were mitigated here in New England by the fact that the slaves were household servants and farm hands, whose masters and mistresses did not themselves disdain the severest toils, so that the servant was brought into closer contact with the master.

I am able to present you here to-day with a document which will make you realize the immense difference between the last century and this century in respect to the sacredness of human personality. It is the original document of sale of a negro girl in this town in the year 1750. The paper was found in an old drawer of the Royce family, and is kindly furnished me by Mrs. Hobert Hull.

"Know all men by these presents that I Joseph Shailer of haddam in the County of Hartford in the Colony of Connecticut in new england do acknowledg my self in plain and open market for and in consideration of the some of one hundred and sixty pounds to have sold and set over unto dec Benjamin Roys of Walingford in New Haven County one negro girl called violet aged about three years to be the sd Benjamin Royses slave and servant and to his heirs and asigns during the full term of her natural life avouching my self to be the proper and sole owner of the sd negro girl and have a Right to dispose of the sd negro girl during the term of her natural life further I do here by Bind my self and Heirs to defend and warant the sd negro girl violet to the sd Roys his heirs and asigns against the lawfull claims of all persons what soever as witness here of I hereunto have set my hand and seal this 20th of April AD 1750

Joseph Shailer

Nehemiah Pratt
Daniel Hoult"

It seems that deacons of churches, and ministers as well, did not esteem it a violation of Christian principle to own and buy and sell negro girls—"violets"—or negro boys and men.

Out of that century many habits of society have been prolonged into the present one, and it has been the task of the Christian church here and elsewhere to prosecute the work of eradicating practices which the pure gospel of Jesus Christ does not fail in the end to expose and condemn.

As its leader in the moral and spiritual work of the opening century the church (Jan. 3, 1803,) called a man of very different type from any who had gone before him. Erastus Ripley was the fourth pastor of the church.* I do not learn that there was any division over his call to the ministerial office here. There seems to have been no question as to his soundness. He was a thoroughly sincere and good man, bold in denouncing sin, not sparing to speak according to his conviction of duty, even at a funeral. He dealt stout blows and frequent blows with the doctrine of election and future punishment. He was a strong writer but a heavy speaker;—a tall, broad-shouldered, heavy man who did not often smile. In the course of his ministry the congregation rapidly diminished. Great numbers joined themselves to other denominations, and at one time it seemed as if the church would become quite extinct. During eleven years he labored under great discouragements. For seventy-four years, or since the days of White-field, it is not known that there had been a general revival of religion.

Out of a sermon celebrating the one hundredth anniversary of the church, preached by Mr. Hinsdale, Mr. Ripley's immediate successor, January 3, 1830, I learn that the pastor of the church, after a period of great mental depression, was seized with a strong conviction that there was to be a revival. The revival came and came in power. At first church prayer-meetings were held consisting of a very few persons, but "their numbers were soon greatly increased." Sinners in different parts of the town were at length aroused and crowded to the place of prayer. The Spirit of God moved over the place bringing one of

*Ordained in the following February over the church, after a church fast.

those mighty seasons which some of you remember
so well,—in which stillness and thoughtfulness per-
vade places of business and homes ; the Word of
God comes to hearts with convincing force ; men
inquire after the way of salvation ; sinners are converted and Christians are lifted into a higher life.
Mr. Hinsdale testifies that the blessed effects of this
season were still visible when he spoke. Such a
work, after so long a period as that intervening since
Whitefield's time, was a great and glorious experience,
and was no doubt sufficient mightily to affect the
currents of life throughout the town. It was thought
by some that one hundred were converted in this
revival. The record shows sixty-five additions to the
church in the year 1815, no doubt in large part the
fruits of this work. But there was a reaction. In
1816 there are but nine persons entered on the record
as new members ; in 1817, none.

Mr. Ripley was dismissed from the pastoral charge
in February, 1822. It is an item of interest that the
salary at this period was only $400. Mr. Ripley's
nature seems to have been well adapted to the strong-
er and severer work of the ministry, but he lacked
social qualities. Children were afraid of him. I
trust it will be deemed at this distant day no lack of
delicacy in me to say so. It is the testimony of those
who were children when he was pastor that in the
homes and in the schools children all feared him. It
is said that our revered brother, now in heaven, Levi
Yale, could not refrain from telling, with a hearty
laugh, how one of the little girls in a district school,
to whom the pastor was talking about dying, turned

to him with a look of pitiful pleading and said: "Please, Mr. God, let me live a little longer."* One of the older members of this church, whom we know only to love, will forgive me if I tell you a story. She avers that Mr. Ripley made her tell a lie. Down in the old district school-house he was passing, as he was wont to do, along the benches talking with the little folks, when he came to Emeline. "Well, Emeline, I hope you say your prayers every night." Emeline was in the habit of saying her prayers, but her conscience told her very plainly that she did not say them every night. She was too frightened to tell the truth; so she whispered out, "Yes, sir." "I hope you tell the truth, Emeline," said the solemn preacher; "you know it would be an awful thing to tell a lie. You must not say you pray every night unless you do. But I hope you do, don't you?" Says Emeline, "Yes, sir." It was awful to tell a lie, but to her child-mind it was more awful still to tell the truth to a minister who stood to her in the place of God, with power to punish all little children that ever forgot to say their prayers. But this pastor, whom the children did not love, was called to a good

---

* It was not so very uncommon for children of those days to think the minister was God. Nor was it always a proof of very great sanctimoniousness in the pastor. My mother, who sat under that remarkable and so-called *eccentric* preacher familiarly known as Parson Mills of Torringford, declares that, as she used to look at him in the dignity of the pulpit (for he was a man of great dignity, though he was often amusing), she believed him to be God. Our venerable brother, pastor Arms, of Norwich, tells me the same thing has happened to him. Those who know his benignant dignity, without reserve, will not attribute it to any severity of manner.

work. One such revival experience as that of 1814 was worth all it cost him. He was afterwards settled in the parish of Goshen, in the town of Lebanon, where his power as a revival preacher was also apparent and bore blessed fruit. He afterwards returned to this place and died here November 16, 1843, at the ripe age of seventy-three years.

In the fall of that year 1822, in which Mr. Ripley was dismissed, and in the month of November, the Rev. Charles J. Hinsdale was settled over a church in which the revival memories of six years ago were still fresh, and in which they were to be repeated before his ministry should close. The church had indeed, in common with many in New England, at this time entered upon a revival period, marked at intervals by great outpourings of God's Spirit. Such seasons came under nearly all the succeeding pastors and preachers down at least to the year 1848, and have been renewed at intervals since. Mr. Hinsdale will be remembered by many of those present here as a man of engaging manners, thoroughly social, in which, as well as in an animated pulpit style, his efficacy as a pastor largely lay. He says of himself in his closing sermon at Blanford, that the great fundamental doctrines of the gospel formed the staple of his preaching. His pastorate was remarkably successful ; the church and congregation increased ; and by his business management, so far as that belongs to a pastor, he doubtless helped much to secure the outward prosperity of the church and society. It was during his ministry that, in the year 1831, this house of worship in its original form was erected, after the old one, built in 1755 just in front of this, having stood for seventy-six years and witnessed the growth of a prosperous community, had become unequal to the demands of the times.

That old church of Revolutionary days, how precious its memories had become! At first, and until 1803, without a steeple, then, for the first time of all churches here, it sent the peal of a bell over these Meriden hills—calling to Sabbath worship and town meetings; tolling the ages of the dead and the solemn march of funeral trains; and ringing, as was often the New England custom, for the farmers' nooning and the evening covering of fire at nine o'clock.

It was built with great cost, sixty by fifty feet, with its high pulpit, of course, and its high single gallery; its floor occupied by great square boxes, or pews, as they were then called, which were meant for times when men had families to fill big pews and gloried in having them. Around the front row of the gallery, all the way around, sat the great choir, which had learned to sing at the winter evening singing-school, and which was large enough when it rose to embrace in its circle the whole congregation.

Such was the old church, in which Mr. Hinsdale preached his last sermon December 5, 1830, the manuscript of which lies before me as I write. I cannot more fitly close this notice of him and his ministry than by quoting from that sermon the following eloquent words. "Seventy-five years ago," said the preacher, "as at this present time, this house was filled with venerable age, vigorous manhood, ardent youth, and restless childhood. Where are they ? Scarce one left to tell the tale. Since that period two generations have gone to join the congregation of the dead. . . . . What tender ties have been severed ! what fond expectations laid prostrate in the dust ! . . . . What keen remembrance flits across the soul as we people again this congregation with the departed ! Does there not seem to come a voice from these crumbling walls, 'For what is your life ? It is even a vapor that appeareth for a little time, then vanisheth away.' "

The new house was finished, and the dedication sermon was preached June 16, 1831. You remember it well, as it stood in its original form till the year 1862, a period of thirty-one years. To that house, which cost about seven thousand dollars, it has interested me, and will interest you, to have discovered the original list of subscribers, and to see from it in what sums the money was raised, and to recall at the same moment some of the leading men in the place.

Two years and a half Mr. Hinsdale preached in the new church when he closed his useful ministry of eleven years ;* and in the following winter of 1833-4 the glory of the Lord filled the house in a revival during the temporary preaching of the Rev. William McLean, from which it is thought some seventy souls dated their conversion. The church was now without a settled pastor for some three years, until the Rev. Arthur Granger accepted the position and was installed in March, 1836. His brief ministry, which

---

* Mr. Hinsdale died at Blanford, Mass. He was killed instantly, being thrown from his carriage, October 17, 1871, aged 76 years.

5*

began with a revival, closed July, 1838, after a period of two years and four months. That Granger pastorate is one of intense interest.

The years from 1837 to 1841, when Mr. Van Buren was president, were years in which the anti-slavery excitement reached some of its most disgraceful features. It was the time when the term, abolitionist, was a reproach, and when mob law and violence, burning of buildings, and dragging men through streets with ropes, as in the case of Garrison in Boston, and even killing, were made arguments to answer the logic of reason and right. Communities were divided, many good men were conservative. Party politics and ambition intensified, as ever, the violence of the contest. Here in Meriden, such men as Levi Yale, Fenner Bush, and Julius Pratt, felt that more ought to be done in agitation of the great question of the day. They procured the use of the basement of this church for a public lecture by the Rev. Mr. Ludlow, of New Haven, whose benevolent face, looking out from that picture on the table, will command your respect and even love. The lecture had been announced from the pulpit, and the hour drew near when it was to be determined whether, under the patronage of some of the most honored men of the town, there could be free speech in Meriden. The excitement was intense, the occasion was important, and the aspect of affairs dangerous. A company of perhaps a hundred and fifty were gathered in that lower room, which then occupied part of the space of the present lecture-room. The speaker had opened his address. when, outside, violent demonstrations begun. The door was locked inside and barricaded. The mob gathered around it and banged it with a battering-ram from a neighboring wood-pile. The door was strong, but there was just cause of alarm to the breathless company inside, who could never know, in those days, to what desperate violence a wild and passionate mob from a neighboring tavern might carry measures against a defenceless company of men and women. The door was opened by those inside, when the company were assaulted with eggs, the common missile of mobs in those days.

The meeting was broken up. Violence was offered and some blows dealt. Those who tried to escape were pelted with stones and eggs, till, as Mr. Ludlow used to declare, he himself "looked like a big pumpkin pie." But noble men like Bush, and Yale, and Pratt, stood by him as a body-guard, walked in the face of the mob and its howling threats and its flying missiles, into the street, some of them escorting him down to the house where Mr. Granger then lived, and which stands next north of the house of Mr. F. T. Ives on Broad street. No one was seriously injured. The coolness of the men protected them. One gentleman and his wife from Berlin were severely treated. Blows were struck,—one knife is said to have been drawn in the confusion. The rioters were successful; mob law had asserted itself. The excitement involved the whole community, and particularly this church, around whose doors the scenes had been enacted, and whose members were divided in their views of expediency on the main question and perhaps even at that time in their sympathies. Arthur Granger did

not like excitement, he had hitherto kept quiet. Now
he spoke for free speech as against the hand of violence. The opposition turned itself against him, and
a mob, born of hell, resulted in the dismissal of a
pastor of the Congregational church in Meriden.
Mr. Granger withdrew. He went to Middletown,
where he was soon settled, and thence to Providence,
R. I., where he also became pastor of a church, in
which office he died after a very short period of
service.

Mr. Granger was a man of very agreeable personal
appearance, stout, with a full but intellectual face,
and, if we may judge from the positions to which he
was soon called, a man of more than usual pulpit
power. He was cautious and averse to disputes. To
this aversion, one, who seems to have known him
intimately, ascribes the readiness with which he left
a pastorate which offered at that time little that could
be attractive to any but a man of strong nerve and
firm will.

For three years the church was without a pastor,
when it secured, in May, 1841, the services of a man
whom no mobs could control and no opposition could
silence. George W. Perkins was the last of that line
of pastors who, from the time of Theophilus Hall,
for a period of nearly one hundred and twenty years,
presided over an undivided church. He was so well
known to many of you that what I say of him here
will seem tame to be said, except to the younger
portion of the audience, who never saw him. He
was a man of remarkable gifts. Of scholarly attain-
ments, he took pride in giving a character of literary

excellence to his productions ; of a pleasant countenance and a genial temper, he knew how to win men ; possessed of strong pulpit power, he commanded the respect of his listeners ; bold of speech, he did not hesitate to emphasize his sentiments ; chastened by affliction, he knew the worth of the gospel of Jesus Christ to the needs of human hearts. It was his strong will and his persuasive power, born of personal magnetism, that held the elements of the church in union through several years of violent moral and political agitations. He was known throughout the State as a strong opponent of slavery. It is said of him by his biographer that he was, on that account, one of the most unpopular men in Connecticut ; but he was a man in whom there was neither sham nor cant,—one of Theophilus Hall's downright honest men,—liberal in his theology and free in his speech, whom no threats nor sneers nor coaxing could silence. His fellow-ministers were tired of hearing him on the old theme of slavery. Yet they respected his ability, and invited him to preach the *Concio ad Clerum* at one of the commencements of Yale College, on the subject of sanctification, into which it was presumed no plea for the slave could be brought. But they had chosen just the right theme for the man. George Perkins rose in his place to speak. " Brethren," said he to the astonished listeners, " the greatest obstacle to sanctification in the church of America is slavery." The church prospered under his ministry, and he enjoyed his life in Meriden, though he was sometimes obliged to confess that a whole year had been spent without a single apparent conversion. It was under

his ministry that the church at length divided. Of
that step the causes lay deeper than human design.
The drift of population towards the railroad, the interests of property-holders, the apparent inclination
of the pastor, acting according to an honest judgment
between the conflicting claims of his friends, all resulted in a final decision,—the temporary excitement
of which has long since died away,—to erect a new
church in West Meriden. The records show at this
distant day to the careful reader a due degree of the
spice of controversy and of conflicting wishes, but
on the whole the division seems to have been wisely
effected. The larger portion of the church went with
the pastor, taking, I believe, one-half the property,
the records of the church, and the fair legal title* to
be called, as they have called themselves, The First
Congregational Church ; while they left to the old
spot a band of noble men and women who would not
desert it ; leaving to that band those memories which

---

* One, whom I have reason to regard as an impartial judge upon
this point, has informed me since the above was written, that this
statement is incorrect. The gentleman, who is in no way connected
with Center church, states that, as the law regulating such matters
then stood, the legal title to the name was never gained by the majority
who went away, but was assumed by the weight of influence. The
circumstances were peculiar. A majority left the old church and the
minority remained. The writer thinks that any one who is in the
habit of attending councils, will readily see at this distant day how
much better it would have been if those who went away had agreed
with those who remained upon a compromise, by which neither party
should claim to be the *First*, and each had adopted some local name,
which would not have perpetuated a vexed question. If such an
arrangement could be made when the other church goes into its new
and elegant place of worship, nothing would more effectually bury the
past and promote Christian harmony.

we are now reviving, hallowed by the associations of
a hundred and twenty years ; leaving to it the echo
of the voices of a whole line of noble pastors, and all
those precious traditions which, once rooted in the
soil, can never be torn away and transplanted. Under
the inspiring shadow of those traditions, over a hundred members grouped themselves around the altar
which their fathers had builded. Some of them were
men of strength, men who had given the weight of
influential characters to this growing town. They
belonged to a generation almost the last of whom
have passed away, mighty men of old.

The remaining church was fortunate in its first
pastor after the division. Asahel A. Stevens, now
of Peoria, Illinois, then a young man, of engaging
manners and pleasant face, if I may judge from the
likeness which lies on the table before me, joined in
pastoral work with Mr. Perkins while the congrega-
tions remained together, and continued in the vacated
place after the division. He remained here until
1854, when, on account of his failing voice, amid the
regrets of an affectionate people, he was dismissed.
He was afterwards invited to return, but was compelled to decline the call. A delightful revival which
came over the church while he was laboring in company with Mr. Perkins, was jealously attributed by
his friends, and doubtless would have been attributed
by his associate, largely to his youthful zeal.

I shall not detain you longer, dear friends, with
details of this later church history. It is well known
to most of you. How greatly you have been prospered above your hopes and faith; with what labors

my predecessor, beloved by so many of you, helped
to build up the church ; and with what sacrifices, in
the past few years, you have enlarged and beautified
this house of your fathers, and how steadily the
church has been and is growing from those days
when a little over a hundred of you banded together
afresh, until now, under God, you are strong in a
membership of about two hundred and sixty souls,
all this, with grateful hearts, ascribe to Him who has
" set before you an open door."

Once more, dear friends, before we step towards
the long century which stretches far away beyond
the mortal reach of any of us, let us turn to greet
the past : the dear and honored names of Hall, and
Hubbard, and Willard, and Ripley, and Hinsdale,
and Perkins, all dead now ; the dear faces of our
forefathers with their noble deeds ; the dear faces of
kindred and friends who have gone up on high.   In
their names, too, let us greet the walls under which
they have gathered before us or with us, and which we
hallow for their sakes.   Once more, with outstretched
arms, let us greet each other, promising to " put on, as
the elect of God, holy and beloved, bowels of mercies,
kindness, humbleness of mind, meekness, long suffer-
ing, forbearing one another, forgiving one another;"
once more let us greet the brethren of the same
household who have gone out from us ; once more the
whole church of God around us ; and upon ourselves
and upon them, with uplifted hands, let us pray: Grace,
mercy, and peace from God our Father, and Jesus
Christ our Lord, Amen.

APPENDIX.

As the foregoing sermons touch only very briefly upon the pastorates which follow that of Mr. Stevens, some of the more important features of the later history of the church, down to the present time. are presented in this Appendix.

Immediately after the dismissal of Mr. Stevens, the church. October 13. 1854, voted to invite the Rev. A. S. Cheesbrough "to supply the pulpit to the 1st January, 1856." Mr. Cheesbrough acted as pastor of the church during that period. At the present time he is preaching in Durham, of this State, where, it is reported, a revival work has been recently developed.

On the 30th December, 1856, the church "voted unanimously to invite Rev. Asahel A. Stevens to return to us, and again become our pastor." This invitation Mr. Stevens, while cherishing for the church "most affectionate and grateful remembrance," was obliged to refuse.

The Rev. Lewis C. Lockwood was installed pastor of the church June 3, 1857. This pastorate was for some reason unfortunate, and Mr. Lockwood was dismissed February 22, 1858, after a period of only eight months.

At a meeting of the church held on the 25th May, 1858, "it was voted unanimously that Rev. O. H. White be invited to become the pastor of this church and society." Mr. White accepted this invitation so far as to become the *acting pastor* of the church, in which relation he continued, without installment, down to the year 1862. Mr. White afterwards went to New Haven, where he labored with the Howard Avenue church, and he is at the present time, or was recently, in England, under an appointment of the American Missionary Association for the Freedmen.

6

The Rev. J. J. Woolley was installed pastor of the church October 22, 1862, in which office he continued until the 14th of August, 1871, at which time, by advice of Council, the pastoral relation was dissolved. Of him, as the immediate predecessor of the writer in the pastoral office, it is due him to say, that his great frankness of manner, his affection for the soldiers in the late war, in which he had acted as chaplain, and his general interest in the welfare of Meriden, won to him a multitude of friends. His name ought to be permanently associated with the granite monument which now stands in front of our City Hall to commemorate the soldiers who died in the Union cause. Largely to his labors we are indebted for that public work.

The church prospered, particularly in the earlier part of his ministry. The membership rose during his pastorate from 176 in 1862, to 212 in 1871—a net increase of 46 persons. Mr. Woolley removed to Pawtucket, in Rhode Island, where he is now settled over an important church, as associate with the Rev. C. Blodgett, D. D.

The present pastor of the church was installed February 15, 1872. Were it not that the writer, in looking up the materials which enter into this history, has learned the importance of completeness in any account which is transmitted to the future, this narrative would terminate here. But if the pastor of this church a hundred years hence, should undertake anew the labor which has now been gone through, he will send his thanks back to his forerunners in these labors for a concise statement of the events of the present pastorate, should this little volume come into his hands.

The parsonage, in the front room of which these lines are being written, was built in the preceding pastorate, largely through the generosity and the labors of Dea. Walter Booth, who gave the land and superintended the building. Very soon after the present pastor was installed, the church and society undertook to enlarge and beautify their house of worship. In this undertaking the foundations were removed from all the western portion of the building; the ground was excavated for a new lecture-room and parlors, and the whole building was extended twenty feet to the west. The interior of the audience-room was thoroughly reconstructed, the galleries were taken down and rebuilt, the present organ was purchased, and the choir removed from the east to the west end of the building. The whole cost of the reconstruction, including decoration and the organ, was about $14,000, the whole of which has been paid. The church has steadily grown until the present time; the net increase being from 213 in 1872, to 263 in this month of March, 1877—a gain of 50.

At the present writing the church is passing through a period of revival, in which the entire city has participated, and the results of which can not yet be determined. The work began in a union of this church with the neighboring First Baptist church, of which the Rev. B. O. True is pastor, the two churches laboring together with the assistance of the Reverend Evangelist A. B. Earle. There have been conversions in all the churches—Christians have been greatly quickened, and a lasting impression, it is believed, has been made upon the city. As the work progressed, the Baptist, Methodist, and Congregational churches united, five in all, assembling together in entire disregard of denominational lines.

At other periods during the past five years the church has seemed to experience a fresh baptism of the Spirit, but in general its history has been one of gradual, and, perhaps, too quiet development. It is a pleasure to write these lines at a time when the church seems, at last, after long years of struggle and of uncertainty, to be established on a firm foundation, and to be entering with fresh hopes on a period of greater prosperity than it has seen since the separation of the majority from it.

The deacons of the church are at the present time as follows: BENJAMIN H. BOYCE, N. B. WOOD, HOBERT H. SMITH, JAMES R. SUTLIFF.

The Members of the Examining Committee, which is also an advisory board along with the pastor, are, besides the above named deacons, David Hobert, Wm. H. Yale, Mrs. H. N. Waters, Dr. John Tait, Miss E. A. Landfear, J. R. French.

The following figures will show the rate of growth of the church since 1848:

Pastorates.	Year.	Males.	Females.	Total.
A. A. Stevens,	1848	44	82	126
"	1849	47	83	130
"	1850	54	98	152
"	1851	55	103	158
"	1852	55	101	156
"	1853	56	100	156
A. S. Cheesbrough,	1854	70	107	177
"	1855	68	109	177
"	1856	61	107	168
L. C. Lockwood,	1857	60	101	161
O. H. White,	1858	58	97	155
"	1859	60	93	153
"	1860	64	102	166
"	1861	69	85	154
J. J. Woolley,	1862	67	109	176
"	1863	68	100	168
"	1864	71	123	194
"	1865	73	130	203
"	1866	73	126	199
"	1867	70	123	193
"	1868	90	152	242
"	1869	80	135	215
"	1870	.81	132	213
"	1871	81	131	212
Edward Hungerford,	1872	78	135	213
"	1873	80	138	218
"	1874	82	161	243
"	1875	86	170	256
"	1876	87	175	262

REV. JOHN HUBBARD'S CONFESSION OF FAITH,

Copied from a printed pamphlet in the Historical Society at Hartford, bearing the following title:

THE TRANSACTIONS OF THE COUNCIL CALLED

FOR THE

ORDINATION OF MR. JOHN HUBBARD,

At MERIDEN, December 29, 1767,

AND THE CONSOCIATION OF THE COUNTY OF NEW HAVEN, CONVENED THERE AT THE SAME TIME.

NEW HAVEN. Printed and sold by THOMAS and SAMUEL GREEN, at their Printing Office in the Old State House.

Mr. Hubbard's Confession of His Christian Faith, Exhibited to the Council.

I believe there is one God supreme, possessed of all possible perfection, excellency, and glory, the Almighty maker of heaven and earth, and that He not only made but constantly exercises a universal providence and superintendency over all the works of His hands. That all things possible are beheld by His all-seeing mind in one view, and that all things are under His absolute control; not a sparrow falls to the ground without our Heavenly Father; and that God worketh all things according to the counsel of His will.

I believe in Jesus Christ, the second person in the blessed Trinity; the brightness of the Father's glory, that being in the form of God He thought it no robbery to be equal with God, and that as He was in the beginning with God, so He was God.

I believe in the Eternal Spirit, or Holy Ghost, the Father underived, the Son begotten of the Father, the Holy Ghost proceeding from the Father and Son, and that they are all possessed of divine power and glory.

I believe that the moral government of God Most High is

6*

absolutely perfect, and His whole administration without error.
That God created all things by Jesus Christ, for the manifesta-
tion of His glorious perfections. I believe that God created
man in His own image, and made him upright, endowed him
with the noble powers of reason and understanding, and placed
him at the head of this lower world ; forbid him to eat of the
fruit of the tree of knowledge of good and evil, upon pain of
death ; that he rebelled against the express prohibition of God,
and judgment came not only upon him, but upon all his pos-
terity to condemnation, and so death passeth upon all, for that
all have sinned ; he being the parent and head of the race, his
transgression was imputed to them, and they suffered the evil
consequences of his transgression, or they were made sinners.
That God did not leave all to perish under the ruins of the
apostacy, but so loved the world that He gave His only begotten
Son, that whosoever believeth in Him should not perish, but
have everlasting life. This glorious and divine Personage, at
the appointment of the Father, when the fullness of time was
come, assumed our nature, taught mankind the way of God in
truth, opened the plan of mercy, the designs of God's grace to
our lost and ignorant race. I believe that He died upon the
cross. an expiation for sin, that the Father laid on Him the
iniquities of us all, and that He bore our sins in His own body
on the tree, offering himself through the Eternal Spirit to God,
without spot, and that the blood of His cross, or His obedience
to death and perfect sacrifice is the meritorious ground upon
which pardon is bestowed upon sinners, or that by Him we
have redemption through His blood, the forgiveness of sin, according to the exceeding riches of God's grace. That He rose
from the dead, ordered that repentance and remission of sin
should be preached to all nations, ascended upon high, received
gifts for men, is seated at the right hand of the Majesty on
high; sent down the Holy Spirit upon the apostles, and ever
lives to make intercession for His people. And as the whole
human race are born of the flesh, and find a law in their members warring against the law of their mind, and bringing them
into captivity to the law of sin, so in order to their eternal salvation by Christ, I believe it is absolutely necessary that they be

regenerated or born again; this moral change I believe is effected by the Spirit of God, through the truth, or that they are born of incorruptible seed by the word of God, which liveth and abideth for ever. The necessary conditions of acceptance on the sinner's part are, repentance towards God, and faith towards our Lord Jesus Christ; in which are included, or from which flow all the graces of Christianity: for the gift and exercise of which they are indebted to God. they are His gifts. Yet in the ordinary method of God's grace, they are obtained by a diligent use of all the means God hath appointed in His Word, and that in the neglect of these we have no warrant from the Word of God to expect the saving blessings of His grace. I believe the necessity of the sanctification of the Spirit, as well as the belief of the truth, in order to our enjoyment of the favor of God hereafter, and the possession of those mansions which Christ by His obedience and death hath purchased, and is now gone to prepare for the heirs of salvation, for without this none shall see God. I believe that all those who are called according to God's purpose, are particularly foreknown and predestinated, and justified upon account of the righteousness of Christ, depended upon by them. and imputed to them, they receiving Him as exhibited to them, as the Lord their righteousness, and they shall be glorified, and that neither death nor life, nor angels, nor principalities, nor powers, nor things present nor things to come, nor height, nor depth, nor any other creature shall be able to separate them from the love of God, which is in Christ Jesus. And in the important business of religion, weak, insufficient man is absolutely dependent upon the influence of the Spirit of God. For it is God that works in us, both to will and to do, and without the grace and strength of Christ, we can do nothing, but through Christ's strengthening of us, we can do all things. And that all necessary grace is purchased by Christ. and freely offered to men with the call of the Gospel: so that all who live ungodly, and die impenitently, must take the blame to themselves, and ascribe their eternal damnation not to any constitution of heaven, or deficiency of God, or the Redeemer, but to their own perverseness and obstinacy; and their own consciences must for ever vindicate the righteousness of God in their perdition, while on the other hand those who by the grace of God comply with the offers of His mercy, will for ever ascribe their salvation to the pure, rich, and unmerited love of God and the grace of our Lord Jesus Christ, who loved them, and washed them in His blood. I believe the resurrection of the dead, and that God hath appointed a day in the which he will judge the world in righteousness, by Jesus Christ, whom He hath ordained judge, both of quick and dead, who will render to every one, according to the deeds done in the body, whether good or bad. That the righteous will be received to glory and the wicked punished with everlasting destruction from the presence of the Lord and the glory of His power. These I take to be taught in God's Holy Word, which I believe to be the only rule for Christians.

MERIDEN, Jan. 1, 1768.

This is the confession of faith read by Mr. John Hubbard, Jr.

Test :   JOHN DEVOTION, Scribe.

Jan. 1, 1768.—After reading and delivering in the foregoing confession of faith, Mr. Hubbard gave answers to questions that were asked him, as follows :

Q. In your confession of faith, speaking of Christ, you say that He was in the beginning with God. What do you mean there, by in the beginning?

Ans. Before all time ; coeval with the Father.

Q. What do you mean by saying, Christ is God ?

Ans. That He is properly a divine person, possessed of divine glory.

Q. What is meant by the Spirit's, or Holy Ghost's, proceeding from the Father and the Son ?

Ans. He proceeds in a manner different from what any creatures do, and in such a manner that he is strictly eternal.

Q. As there are Three Persons in the Godhead, are they all properly speaking One God?

Ans. Yes.

Q. How are we sinners by Adam's transgression ? Is it

as we stand related to him as the head of the family? and so do we derive from him family or relative guilt?

Ans. Yes.

Q. Do you believe that in consequence of the sovereign judgment of God, whereby we are all subjected to death, all mankind would have been finally ruined and for ever lost, if a Mediator had not been provided?

Ans. Yes.

Q. Do you believe that if any of the human race are delivered from this state of guilt, condemnation, and death, it is by the sovereign grace of God, on account of the righteousness of Christ?

Ans. Yes.

Q. Do you suppose that the present state of human nature is such, that without the influence of the Spirit and grace of God we should live and grow up in wickedness, and finally perish?

Ans. Yes.

Q. Do you suppose that these influences of the Spirit would have been given to any if it had not been for the purchase of Christ?

Ans. No.

Q. By liberty do you mean that we have a natural and practical ability to do all that is required of us in order to salvation, without the special influence of the Spirit of God?

Ans. No. By saying we have liberty of will, I mean no more than that we have such liberty as to constitute us moral agents and accountable creatures.

Q. Do you believe that by the new covenant and promise of God saints have secured to them all that is necessary to their perseverance and final salvation?

Ans. Yes.

Q. Do you suppose the promise of God is so to be understood as to secure assistance in the neglect of duty?

Ans. No.

Q. Do you suppose the good works of believers are the ground of their right and title to eternal life?

Ans. No.

Q. Are the good works of believers the ground of their election to eternal life ?

Ans. No. But the mere grace and mercy of God.

Q. Do you believe that any works done, or that can be done, by natural men, are accepted as gracious works?

Ans. No.

Q. What do you understand by regeneration, or conversion ?

Ans. It is a change of both heart and life from sin to holiness by the influence of the Spirit of God.

Q Is there an inward change previously necessary to the performance of good works acceptable to God ?

Ans. Yes.

Q. Do you not suppose that God has predetermined the final condemnation of impenitent sinners in consequence of His foresight of their willful wickedness ?

Ans. Yes.

Q. Does not true faith include (over and above an assent to gospel truth) a dependence upon Christ for salvation ?

Ans. Yes.

Q. How is this faith wrought ? Is it not by the influence of the Spirit of God given by Christ ?

Ans. Yes.

Q. Tho' it is by the influence of the Spirit of God that any are enabled truly to believe and do works spiritually good, yet does this destroy moral agency ?

Ans. No.

These are the questions asked by the council, and answers given by Mr. Hubbard, in the audience of a large concourse, with full liberty, publicly offered to any, to ask any other questions, or to have an explanation of those already asked.

Test :   JOHN DEVOTION, Scribe.

The council (besides the foregoing transactions with the consociation), having received particular and full information of the state of the church and society in Meriden, came to the following result on Friday evening, Jan. 1, viz:

That altho' in our opinion, it is the undoubted and unaliena-
ble right of every church to choose their own pastor, or in-
structor, in righteousness, and altho' Mr. Hubbard appears
to be well qualified to do service in the churches of our Lord
Jesus Christ, both as to his abilities and religious sentiments,
(so far as we have been acquainted with them by his examination and confession of faith) if he should be improved therein ;
yet, considering the broken and divided state of this church
and society, and other unhappy circumstances, we don't see
our way clear to proceed to his ordination at present.

Passed in council

Test: JOHN DEVOTION.)
JOHN WHITING, } Scribes.

This is, I believe, the first time that the above confession
and examination of John Hubbard have been reproduced. It
has been a matter of great interest to learn, over what *heresy*
this church and the colony were so long kept in turmoil. The
supposition, offered in the second of the foregoing sermons,
that there was nothing in Mr. Hubbard's belief which would
render him unacceptable to any congregation of ordinary intelligence at the present day, seems to be fully confirmed by the
discovery of this document. The Confession of Faith is pre-
ceded in the pamphlet by the correspondence between the
consociation and the council. The council met at " Madam
Hall's," probably meaning the home of Theophilus Hall's
widow, on the present Avery Hall place. The consociation met
at some place not specified, but two miles distant from the
council.

BASIS OF CHURCH MEMBERSHIP.

At a church meeting held May 1, 1873, it was voted, with but one dissenting voice, to do away with the previously existing doctrinal basis of church membership, and to substitute for it the following

FORM OF CHRISTIAN PROFESSION AND COVENANT,

to which, alone, applicants for admission to the church are required, after examination by the committee and acceptance by vote of the church, to give consent :

CHRISTIAN PROFESSION.

In presenting yourself (yourselves) for membership in Christ's Church, you do now publicly profess your hearty faith in God, who is revealed to us in the gospel as Our Father in Heaven ; and in Jesus Christ His only begotten Son -the Saviour of the world,—who died for our transgressions and rose again from the dead, and humbly confessing your sins, you do now in the presence of these witnesses solemnly avow the consecration of yourself (yourselves) to God and His service in the observance of all His commandments as set forth in His Holy Word ; depending on the gracious influences of His Spirit for your comfort and strengthening in all godliness.

COVENANT WITH THE CHURCH.

You do also covenant to walk with this Church in christian fellowship and in the conscientious performance of the mutual obligations of its members and in the ordinances which Christ has enjoined to be observed by His people. You engage to be subject to the discipline of Christ's Church in general and this in particular, so long as God continues you here.

RECEPTION BY THE CHURCH.

We then, the Church of Christ in this place, declare you to be a member of Christ's Church in general, and this in particular ; and promise by divine help to treat you with such affection and watchfulness as your sacred relation to us requires. This we promise, imploring of our Lord that both we and you may obtain mercy to be faithful in his covenant and glorify Him by the holiness which becometh His house for ever.

DATE OF ORGANIZATION.

The following Preamble and Resolution, setting forth the facts relating to the date of organization of this church, were adopted in a full meeting of the church, held on Easter Sunday, April 1, 1877 :

WHEREAS, At the time of the separation of the majority from this church, in the year 1848, a strong pressure was brought to bear upon this church to induce it to yield its title to be considered a church without a new organization, as is shown by the following resolutions passed at different times and entered upon the records, as also by an act of the council ordaining the Rev. A. A. Stevens pastor over this church, which resolutions and act of council are as follows, namely :

" At a meeting of brethren of the Congregational Church in Meriden, held in the basement of their church on the 13th day of January, 1848, the following preamble and resolution were presented and passed unanimously :

" WHEREAS, A majority of this church, together with the pastor, have left us and taken the church records ; therefore,

"*Resolved,* That in consequence thereof, the regular administration of public worship and religious ordinances will not be suspended in this house ; but that we who remain, now proceed with our present 'Confession of Faith and Covenant,' in all church duties and ordinances: "

this preamble and resolution being marked upon the record as "rescinded Jan. 24," and the action of the next meeting being recorded as follows :

" Monday, Jan. 24, 1848.

" The brethren of the church met agreeable to vote of the last meeting.

" The first preamble and resolution passed at the last meeting were reconsidered and rescinded, and the following preamble and resolution were passed unanimously :

" WHEREAS, A majority of this church have voted to remove to their new meeting-house, and the pastor has given notice to that effect, and also given notice that his relation as pastor to us who remain has closed, therefore,

"*Resolved*, That we still are a Church of Christ; and though for substantial reasons we waive our rights as being THE Congregational Church of Meriden, and we hereby assume the name of, and will hereafter be known as, the Center Congregational Church of Meriden, and still holding to our church 'Covenant and Confession of Faith,' will go forward with the ordinances regularly administered: "

this resolution not having been rescinded, the record goes on as follows :

"Another meeting was called Feb. 17, 1848. The following preamble and vote were then passed :

" WHEREAS, A majority of the Congregational Church of Meriden have built and occupied their new house of worship, and whereas the former house is preferable to us, therefore,

"*Resolved*, That we who remain to worship in the old house, do associate and proceed as a Church of Christ, by the name of the Center Congregational Church of Meriden, with the present 'Covenant and Confession of Faith,' to sustain all church duties and ordinances."

"The above resolution was passed in consideration of the following declaration of the pastor of the Congregational Church :

" If the preceding vote should be passed, I should feel authorized to comply with the wishes of those who assent to it, and enter their names on our record as having their connection with us terminated.   G. W. PERKINS."

"March 15, 1848.

"At an Ecclesiastical Council convened at the house of the Center Congregational Church, by letters missive from the Center Congregational Church in Meriden, to take into consideration the expediency of ordaining to the gospel ministry Mr. Asahel A. Stevens, an inquiry was then made by the council into the authority of the brethren calling this council to act as a Church of Christ : whereupon it was resolved that in view of the following act of organization, without reference to any previous documents, viz :

" WHEREAS a majority of the Congregational Church of Meriden have built and occupied their new house of worship, and whereas the former house is preferable to us ; therefore,

"*Resolved*, That we who remain to worship in the old house do associate and proceed as a Church of Christ, by the name of the Center Congregational Church of Meriden, with the present 'Covenant and Confession of Faith,' to sustain all church duties and ordinances."

"This council recognize the brethren so agreeing as having thereby become a duly organized Church of Christ."

And WHEREAS, From the first two resolutions, and from the ambiguous language of the third resolution, in which the non-ecclesiastical term "associate," is carefully chosen as an ambiguous term, agreed upon by the parties purposely to avoid the usual word "organize," it is evident that this church regarded itself as never having ceased to be a church since the original organization in 1729;

And WHEREAS, By the concurrent testimony of those still living among us, who were conversant with the doings of that time, and some of whom were present at the council, it appears that the church had not previous to the council conceded—nor did it, notwithstanding the language of the council (which language was purely the council's own, and in no way binding upon the church), at the time of the council concede, nor has it since conceded that it has ever ceased to be a church, nor has it ever had an organization since 1729:

Therefore, in the light of this history, and for the information of the public,

Resolved, That we do as did our fathers, date the organization of this church from the year of our Lord. 1729.

Attest:

GEO. E. FLINT, Clerk.